PRIMARIES
★ AND ★
CONVENTIONS

PRIMARIES AND CONVENTIONS

★ ROY HOOPES ★

FRANKLIN WATTS
NEW YORK | LONDON | 1978
AN !MPACT BOOK

Cartoons courtesy of:

Sidney Harris: pp. 16, 29, 32, 45, 57, 76; Rothco Cartoons: (Pearson-Knickerbocker News) p. 43, (Audley-London Sunday Telegraph) p. 52, (Valtman) p. 62.

Chart courtesy of: League of Women Voters: pp. 22–27.

Library of Congress Cataloging in Publication Data

Hoopes, Roy, 1922–
Primaries and conventions.

(An Impact book)
Bibliography: p.
Includes index.
SUMMARY: Explains the process by which Presidential and Vice-Presidential candidates are nominated and discusses the role of campaign financing, primaries, caucuses, and conventions.
1. Presidents—United States—Nomination—Juvenile literature. 2. Primaries—United States—Juvenile literature. 3. Political conventions—Juvenile literature. [1. Presidents—Election. 2. Political conventions. 3. Politics, Practical] I. Title.
JK521.H66 329'.022'0973 77-17468
ISBN 0-531-01356-1

Printed in the United States of America
6 5 4 3 2 1

★ CONTENTS ★

PRIMARIES ★ AND ★ CONVENTIONS

★ INTRODUCTION ★

The President of the United States is the most powerful elected official in the world. In fact, in recent years, many students of government in America have been asking: Is the President of the United States too powerful?

How does one person, out of more than 200 million Americans, become a candidate for such a powerful office? How does he obtain the nomination of one of the two political parties that have nominated every President since the Civil War? How is the Vice-Presidential candidate of a political party nominated? What happens at a party's Presidential convention? Could a woman run for the Presidency?

The purpose of this book is to answer these questions. It will explain the process in which Presidential and Vice-Presidential candidates are nominated today and how a Presidential Convention is organized and functions. In doing so, it will help explain what takes place in our political system every four years—prior to the general Presidential campaign. Discussed will be such areas as what primaries and caucuses are and why they are important; why the New Hampshire primary always comes first; what a "front-runner" is; how a Presidential candidate can "win" a primary and still "lose" it; what "keynote speakers," "favorite sons," and the "World Series" of the primaries are; what delegate-hunting is; what is meant by "affirmative action"; why some politicians are criticizing our primary system and why more and more people are talking about "regional" primaries; what is meant by the "power of incumbency"; who picks the city where a Presidential convention is held and by what criteria are the particular cities picked; what is a "dark horse"; what is meant by a "brokered" convention and what goes on in the "smoke-filled rooms."

Students of American government have commented on how well our political system has performed in producing good Presidents and how the system's choices have so often reflected the mood of the American people. More often than not, our Presidential nominating process has picked the right men for the times, which is why more than one student of government has commented on "the genius of American politics."

The process by which the delegates to the Presidential conventions are picked is different in both major political parties and in all fifty states. It is a complicated system and it is constantly being changed and reformed by the political parties and the states. But throughout the years the goals of the reformers have been to make the process by which a Presidental candidate is selected more and more democratic. Hence, it should not only be the responsibility of every American to know and understand the system that picks the person who ultimately will become President, but to take part in that process when he or she becomes old enough to hand out party literature or lick envelopes—and old enough to vote in a Presidential primary, which is eighteen.

CHAPTER 1

ORIGINS

The Constitution says nothing about political parties or how our candidates for the office of the Presidency should be nominated. The Constitution called for a President to be elected by an "Electoral College." The College would be made up of a group of prominent citizens from each state, equal in number to the total number of Senators and Representatives in that state, who would be chosen in *any* way a state might prefer—by the people, by the governor, or by the state legislature. The Founding Fathers were still worried about "mob rule" and the violence of the French Revolution, and they wanted to make certain that the "mob" would not pick our President, unless the government preferred it that way. "Many of the founders," wrote David Cushman Coyle, one of the nation's leading authorities on the origins of the American political system, "thought of the President as sort of an elected King, who would stand above parties like the present-day President of France or King of England." They remembered the bitter struggle between the Whigs and the Tories in the American Revolution and were afraid of political parties. In fact, our first President, George Washington, warned his fellow countrymen, in his famous Farewell Address on leaving the Presidency in 1796, not to trust political parties.

However, in the early days of the nation, it quickly became obvious that political parties were essential in nominating and electing a President. Two principal parties emerged after George Washington's two terms in office—the Federalists, representing business people, finance, and the middle-class city people; and the "Republicans," led by Thomas Jefferson, who represented the farmers and the mountaineers. Incidentally, these Republicans were in no way related to the Republican party that developed in the mid-nineteenth century and still exists today. The Federalists, after nominating and electing John Adams in 1796, began to fade away and were gone by 1820. The Republicans elected

Thomas Jefferson in 1800. But after the disappearance of the Federalists, they began to split into two factions—the National Republicans, led by John Quincy Adams, and the Democratic-Republicans, led by the followers of Thomas Jefferson. They eventually nominated Andrew Jackson as their Presidential candidate in 1828.

The National Republicans represented, essentially, the conservative members of each community, and they were succeeded in 1832 by the Whigs. The Whigs nominated conservative politicians until the mid-1850s, when they began to split over the issue of slavery. The Democratic-Republican party, which by this time was called simply the Democratic party, was also splitting over the issue of slavery. Finally a new anti-slavery party—the Republican party—emerged in 1854 and eventually nominated Abraham Lincoln as its Presidential candidate. Lincoln was elected and served as President during the Civil War, which was fought over the question of whether a state had the right to resolve such issues as slavery within their own legislatures.

After the Civil War, the Democratic and Republican parties came to dominate American politics and have nominated every President elected since then. Of course, from time to time, third parties have nominated serious candidates for the Presidency. Third parties usually have developed when the nation was deeply divided over an issue, and neither of the two major parties took positions that satisfied the people who felt most strongly about the controversial issue. The Republican party originated as a "third party." The Populist party was very powerful for a while in the 1890s. In 1912, former Republican President Theodore Roosevelt formed the Bull Moose party, which helped defeat Republican William Howard Taft and elect Democrat Woodrow Wilson because many Republicans voted for Roosevelt. In 1924, Senator Robert M. La Follette, Sr., of Wisconsin, formed the Progressive party, which was opposed to the big corporations dominating America. He ran for President and received 17 percent of the vote, mostly from the Democrats, a factor in the election of Republican Calvin Coolidge. Former Vice-President Henry Wallace formed another Progressive party in 1948 out of the extreme liberal wing of the Democratic party. That same year a "fourth party," known as the Dixiecrats, was formed by Senator Strom Thurmond out of the extreme conservative wing of the Democratic party. Despite the defections, the Democrats, under Harry S. Truman, surprised everyone by winning the election. More recently, George Wallace, governor of Alabama, ran for President as the candidate of the American Independent party, in 1968 and 1972, and then decided to seek the Democratic nomination in 1976.

However, the two major parties have dominated national politics since the Civil War. And one of the reasons they are so important in American politics is their role in nominating and helping to elect the President. From the late nineteenth century (the era of big city machine politics) to 1932, when Franklin Roosevelt was elected during the Great Depression, the political party was one of the most important institutions in the country. The big city political bosses, for all their corruption and abuses of power, performed many functions that were necessary to the community. They were a combination welfare and employment agency. John Gilligan, former Democratic governor of Ohio and a research scholar who studied the evolution of our political system, has written of this period: "If a citizen needed a job, or wanted to get his wife into the hospital, or his son out of jail, he knew his precinct captain would provide whatever help he could. And [he] asked in return nothing more than every vote in the family."

It was a good bargain. The private citizen was able to obtain the kind of help that wasn't available anywhere else in our society. He also became involved in a social structure in which he played a role. And through his membership in the party, he participated to some extent in the political system that ran his community. In such a system, the political boss became a powerful figure. And he became even more powerful every four years, because he also played an important role in selecting who would represent his state at the national convention that would nominate his party's Presidential candidate.

After 1932, the power of the political boss as a social welfare leader began to wane. With the country in economic chaos, President Roosevelt launched a series of welfare programs that would do for the average citizen in the city and on the farm the kind of things the local political leaders used to take responsibility for. And these programs were continued and expanded under Democratic Presidents Harry Truman, John F. Kennedy, and Lyndon Johnson. However, while losing his social and economic power, the local leader retained his political power because he still played a critical role in the nomination of his party's Presidential and Vice-Presidential candidates. In fact, since 1932, the principal national role of the state political party has been to nominate Presidential candidates and, until very recently, the party bosses controlled that power.

CHAPTER

2

REFORMING THE SYSTEM

To understand how the Presidential and Vice-Presidential candidates of a political party are nominated, it is necessary to know something about the history of political reform in the United States. This reform has been one long struggle to give more and more people the vote and more and more people the right to participate in the nomination of the people being voted for.

The Founding Fathers tried to limit politics and voting to white male property owners. And the Senate of the United States was to be made up of men elected by the state legislatures. Gradually, as the people moved west and new frontier states were admitted to the Union, the democratization of politics evolved. By 1860, almost all white males over the age of twenty-one could vote. After the Civil War, blacks were given the *right* to vote. But the southern states made it difficult for them to exercise that right. It was not until the 1950s, that the Supreme Court struck down the legal obstacles that kept blacks from voting. In 1913, an amendment to the Constitution provided that members of the Senate be elected directly by the people. In 1920, women were given the vote. And in 1970, the legal voting age was lowered to eighteen.

A similar movement to broaden participation in the nominating process has been taking place, but even more gradually. For most of the nation's history, while more and more people were winning the right to vote, the power to nominate the people being voted for was retained by a small, powerful group of white males in each state—the politicians and the representatives of special interest groups, such as business and labor leaders, who often controlled the politicians. These were the "kingmakers," the politicians who got together in "smoke-filled rooms" at political meetings (known as caucuses) and at conventions to nominate the candidates—for governor, for the House of

Representatives, for the Senate, and for the Presidency and Vice-Presidency.

At first the nominations for President were made solely by members of Congress, who met in caucuses to choose their candidates. Then, other party leaders in the state demanded a part. In 1824, the Democratic-Republican caucus failed to nominate Andrew Jackson as the candidate and there was a revolt against the caucus system. In 1828, Jackson supporters attacked "King Caucus" as undemocratic because it was a closed group. Jackson was nominated in 1828, but the caucus was dead as a means of nominating Presidential candidates. In 1832, state party leaders met in local conventions to elect representatives to the state conventions, who, in turn, elected representatives to the national conventions, which nominated the President and Vice-President. This broadened participation in the nomination process because party workers were allowed a voice in picking the candidates.

However, there was still dissatisfaction with the process because the average person who did not take part in party politics did not have a say in nominating the candidates they would ultimately have to decide on at the polls. Near the end of the nineteenth century, a strong movement developed for the adoption of primary elections to elect political candidates—especially for the Presidency. One of the leaders of this movement was Governor and later Senator Robert M. La Follette, Sr., of Wisconsin. In a speech in 1897, La Follette argued for the abolition of both the caucus and conventions, which have "no purpose further than to give respectable form to political robbery." La Follette urged that we "go back to the first principles of Democracy; go back to the people. Substitute for both the caucus and the convention a primary election. . . ."

In 1901, Florida adopted an optional primary law. In 1905, Wisconsin adopted the first state primary election, and the idea of voting directly for a Presidential nominee began to catch on. By 1976, twenty-nine states and the District of Columbia had primaries; the rest chose delegates to the national convention at either political caucus, state convention, or both.

However, despite the increased use of primaries to pick the delegates to the national convention, the political pros —usually white males—managed to retain control of the process in both parties. And this created a crisis in the Democratic party in 1968. In the early primary elections that year, it became obvious that President Lyndon Johnson had strong opposition within his own party, mainly due to the unpopular Vietnam war. In fact, Minnesota Senator Eugene McCarthy did so well in the New Hampshire primary running against Johnson and the war that New York Senator Robert Kennedy finally decided to enter the race. And when Kennedy entered, President Johnson announced that he would not be a candidate and threw his support to his Vice-President, Hubert Humphrey.

Robert Kennedy was gaining popularity and strong support all during the primaries, but he was assassinated while in California for that state's primary. At the convention, held in Chicago, the antiwar forces rallied around Senators McCarthy and George McGovern. But the convention proved to be in the hands of the party professionals, particularly Chicago Mayor Richard J. Daley, who brought about the nomination of Hubert Humphrey, despite the obvious opposition to the Vice-President.

After Humphrey's defeat in the Presidential election, a strong movement developed within the Democratic party to reform the nominating process. The reformers wanted to take it out of the hands of the party regulars. Senator George McGovern was appointed head of a commission that would give young people, women, Chicanos, and blacks greater representation at the 1972 convention, to be held in

"THE WAY I SEE IT, IF I DO WELL IN THE NEW HAMPSHIRE PRIMARY, I CAN GO BACK THERE SOMEDAY AND RUN FOR GOVERNOR."

Miami. Among other things, the McGovern Commission recommended the "quota system," which specified that each state delegation to the convention should have a number of blacks, women, youth, and minorities, in a reasonable relationship to the numbers in their state. In the opinion of most Democrats and non-Democrats alike, the "quota system" went too far. As one Democratic governor said of the Miami Convention: "It looked like the cast from *Hair*" (the popular Broadway musical).

This led to the creation, at the convention, of new commissions to further reform the nominating process and draw up a party charter, which would serve as a guide for all Democratic state parties. The charter was adopted at a midterm conference held in Kansas City, Missouri, in 1974.

The reforms embodied in the charter abolished the quota system and replaced it with "affirmative action" programs designed to broaden participation in party affairs. The charter also abolished the "winner-take-all primaries" and the "unit rule," which enabled a Presidential candidate who had a majority of the delegates in a state to win all of that state's delegate votes at the convention. Finally, the charter created a Compliance Review Commission, which has the power to see that state parties take positive and provable steps to observe the new rules. And it has the power to expel from the convention the delegates of any state that does not comply.

The net result of these reforms was a virtual revolution in the Democratic party's nominating process. As former Ohio Governor John Gilligan, who was very active in the reform movement, says: "It seems remarkable how many people have failed to understand the historic significance of the changes that have taken place in the Democratic Party since 1968. We, the oldest and largest political organization on earth, have done what no other political party in this country or anywhere else in the world has done. We have made a covenant with the people in which we have said that we were going to guarantee that every citizen in the country who wanted to participate in our party could do so, and that any constituent element of our party that violates this pact, risks expulsion."

CHAPTER

3

STATE PRIMARIES AND PARTY CAUCUSES

An important fact to remember about the system of nominating a Presidential candidate is that it is continually being changed and reformed. The system, as a whole, is also extremely difficult and complicated to understand. The reason is that every state has different rules, and each political party's nominating process is different in each of the fifty states. In many states the rules and regulations, which are established either by state law or party rules, are so complicated that even many of the political workers in that state do not understand them.

Essentially, what we call the "primary campaign" in American politics is the effort made by Presidential candidates to win the support of the people chosen to go to the national convention to pick the party's Presidential and Vice-Presidential candidates. These people are "delegates" to the national convention, and each party picks delegates in different ways. Some are picked by primary elections, with people in each political district voting either directly for a Presidential candidate or for delegates who have expressed their preference for a certain candidate. Other states pick their delegates through a series of meetings attended by party members. And in some states, both methods are used—that is, some delegates are picked by a primary election and others are picked by the caucus method.

There are also different kinds of primaries and different kinds of delegates. Most delegates represent a specific precinct or district. But some states have "delegates-at-large," meaning they represent the entire state, rather than a particular district.

The following shows, state by state, the types of primaries, the dates, and the number of delegates selected by each party for the 1976 conventions. This information changes each Presidential election year, but it demonstrates the wide variety of methods used in selecting delegates.

State by State Delegate Selection

KEY

Primary Type	PR/Proportional; WTA/Winner-Take-All; DDS/Direct Delegate Selection; A/Advisory. (Approximately 75 percent of delegates in both parties are selected from states with primaries.)
Other	Congressional District Convention, State Convention, State Committee, Delegate Caucus or other variation
( )	Number of delegates "controlled" by primary. Most delegates actually selected elsewhere.
o	Delegates' Presidential preferences not listed on ballot (WV; NY, PA—Republicans).
*	Democrats allow any state to send at least 16 *delegates* even if the state is entitled to fewer *votes.* Actual votes are: AK/10; DE/12; NV/11; ND/13; VT/12; WY/10. The Canal Zone, Guam, Virgin Islands and Democrats Abroad get 6 delegates, but only 3 votes each.

STATE	PRIMARY		OTHER	
	Type	Dels.	Date	Dels.
ALABAMA				
D-35	DDS	27	May 4	8
R-37	DDS	37	May 4	—
ALASKA				
D-16*	—			16
R-19	—			19
ARIZONA				
D-25	—			25
R-29	—			29
ARKANSAS				
D-26	PR	(26)	May 25	26
R-27	PR	(27)	May 25	27
CALIFORNIA				
D-280	PR	(280)	June 8	280
R-167	WTA	(167)	June 8	167
COLORADO				
D-35	—			35
R-31	—			31
CONNECTICUT				
D-51	—			51
R-35	—			35
DELAWARE				
D-16*	—			16
R-17	—			17
DISTRICT OF COLUMBIA				
D-17	PR	13	May 4	4
R-14	WTA	14	May 4	—
FLORIDA				
D-81	PR	(81)	March 9	81
R-66	WTA	(66)	March 9	66
GEORGIA				
D-50	A,DDS	38	May 4	12
R-48	WTA	(48)	May 4	48

STATE		PRIMARY		OTHER
	Type	Dels.	Date	Dels.
HAWAII				
D-17	—			17
R-19	—			19
IDAHO				
D-16	PR	(13)	May 25	3
R-21	PR	(17)	May 25	4
ILLINOIS				
D-169	A,DDS	155	March 16	14
R-101	A,DDS	96	March 16	5
INDIANA				
D-75	PR	(75)	May 4	75
R-54	WTA	(54)	May 4	54
IOWA				
D-47	—			47
R-36	—			36
KANSAS				
D-34	—			34
R-34	—			34
KENTUCKY				
D-46	PR	(46)	May 25	46
R-37	PR	(37)	May 25	37
LOUISIANA				
D-41	DDS	32	May 1	9
R-41	—			41
MAINE				
D-20	—			20
R-20	—			20
MARYLAND				
D-53	A,DDS	40	May 18	13
R-43	WTA	24	May 18	19
MASSACHUSETTS				
D-104	PR	(104)	March 2	104
R-43	PR	(43)	March 2	43
MICHIGAN				
D-133	PR	(133)	May 18	133
R-84	PR	(84)	May 18	84

STATE	PRIMARY			OTHER
	Type	Dels.	Date	Dels.
MINNESOTA				
D-65	—			65
R-42	—			42
MISSISSIPPI				
D-24	—			24
R-30	—			30
MISSOURI				
D-71	—			71
R-49	—			49
MONTANA				
D-17	PR	(17)	June 1	17
R-20	A		June 1	20
NEBRASKA				
D-23	A,DDS	23	May 11	—
R-25	A,DDS	25	May 11	—
NEVADA				
D-16*	PR	(16)	May 25	16
R-18	PR	(18)	May 25	18
NEW HAMPSHIRE				
D-17	A,DDS	17	Feb 24	—
R-21	A,DDS	21	Feb 24	—
NEW JERSEY				
D-108	A,DDS	91	June 8	17
R-67	A,DDS	67	June 8	—
NEW MEXICO				
D-18	—			18
R-21	—			21
NEW YORK				
D-274	DDS	206	April 6	68
R-154	DDS	117*	April 6	37
NORTH CAROLINA				
D-61	PR	(61)	March 23	61
R-54	PR	(54)	March 23	54

STATE		PRIMARY		OTHER
	Type	Dels.	Date	Dels.
NORTH DAKOTA				
D-16*	—			16
R-18	—			18
OHIO				
D-152	DDS	152	June 8	—
R-97	DDS	97	June 8	—
OKLAHOMA				
D-37	—			37
R-36	—			36
OREGON				
D-34	PR	(34)	May 25	34
R-30	PR	(30)	May 25	30
PENNSYLVANIA				
D-178	A,DDS	134	April 27	44
R-103	A,DDS	85°	April 27	18
RHODE ISLAND				
D-22	PR	18	June 1	4
R-19	PR	19	June 1	—
SOUTH CAROLINA				
D-31	—			31
R-36	—			36
SOUTH DAKOTA				
D-17	PR	13	June 1	4
R-20	PR	20	June 1	—
TENNESSEE				
D-46	PR	37	May 25	9
R-43	WTA	24	May 25	19
TEXAS				
D-130	DDS	98	May 1	32
R-100	DDS	96	May 1	4
UTAH				
D-18	—			18
R-20	—			20

STATE	PRIMARY			OTHER
	Type	Dels.	Date	Dels.
VERMONT				
D-16*	A		March 2	16
R-18	A		March 2	18
VIRGINIA				
D-54	—			54
R-51	—			51
WASHINGTON				
D-53	—			53
R-38	—			38
WEST VIRGINIA				
D-33	A,DDS	25°	May 11	8
R-28	A,DDS	28°	May 11	—
WISCONSIN				
D-68	PR	(68)	April 6	68
R-45	WTA	(45)	April 6	45
WYOMING				
D-16*	—			16
R-17	—			17
CANAL ZONE				
D-6*	—			6
R-0	—			—
GUAM				
D-6*	—			6
R-4	—			4
PUERTO RICO				
D-22	—			22
R-8	—			8
VIRGIN ISLANDS				
D-6*	—			6
R-4	—			4
DEMOCRATS ABROAD-6*	—			6

TOTALS: Democrats: 3048 delegates—3008 votes; Republicans: 2259 delegates and votes

THE CAUCUS-CONVENTION METHOD

Many states select delegates to the national convention at a state convention. But first the members of the party hold a series of caucuses at local precinct or district levels. At these meetings, the party members pick delegates to a county caucus. Then at the county caucus, the party members pick delegates to a state caucus, usually called a state convention. At the state convention, those attending will pick the delegates to the national convention. At each level of caucusing, the supporters of a Presidential candidate (and sometimes even the candidate, if it is an important state) will be trying to persuade the party workers attending the meeting to vote for that candidate.

The party "regulars" tend to favor the caucus method because it gives the party professionals more control over the delegate selection process. To make certain that the wishes of the people in an area are carried out, the rules of the Democratic party specify that the delegates picked at each level to attend a convention should "fairly reflect" the feeling in that district or precinct about preferences for Presidential candidates. In other words, if, say, half the district is for candidate A, one-quarter for candidate B and one-quarter uncommitted, then approximately 50 percent of the delegates to the county or state conventions should favor candidate A, 25 percent candidate B, and 25 percent go uncommitted.

PRIMARIES

In 1976, twenty-nine states and the District of Columbia picked their delegates to the national conventions by primary elections. And the prospect is for even more primaries in the future. A primary election is an election in which the people of a district or precinct vote directly for a Presidential candidate or for the delegates to the national con-

"HOW BINDING ARE CAMPAIGN PROMISES
MADE ONLY IN PRIMARIES?"

vention. There are basically three types of primaries: winner-take-all; proportional; and advisory.

1. **Winner-take-all:** In this type of primary, the candidate who receives the most votes in the state elections wins all the delegates to the national convention. Let us say that a state has twenty-seven delegates to the convention. In the primary, candidate A gets 38 percent of the votes; candidate B gets 20 percent; candidate C gets 13 percent; candidate D gets 10 percent; and 19 percent of the people vote to send uncommitted delegates to the convention. In the winner-take-all primary, candidate A would get 100 percent —all twenty-seven of the delegates that state sends to the national convention.

2. **Proportional:** In the proportional primary, the delegates to the national convention are selected in direct proportion to the number of votes received by each candidate. Thus, in the above example, of the twenty-seven delegates to the national convention, candidate A would get 38 percent of the delegates; candidate B, 20 percent; candidate C, 13 percent; candidate D, 10 percent; and 19 percent would go uncommitted.

3. **Advisory:** A few states have what are called "advisory" primaries, which politicians and reporters call "beauty contests." These primaries do not actually pick any delegates. They merely permit voters to express their preferences, which theoretically provides guidance to the people who will actually pick the delegates to the national convention at the party caucuses and state conventions.

The rules for placing a candidate's name on the ballot for a primary election vary from state to state. However, state rules cannot prevent anyone eligible under the Constitution from running in a state. To be eligible for the Presidency, a person must be at least thirty-five years of age, an American citizen born in the United States or of American parents living abroad and have lived in the United States at least fourteen years.

The dates on which primary elections and state conventions are held also vary from state to state. If there is a primary, a candidate's name must be filed with state election officials by a certain date, usually two months before the primary date. It is also possible in some states for supporters of a Presidential candidate who is not on the ballot to organize a "write-in" campaign for that candidate. Both parties award delegates to the convention in proportion to the number of write-in votes they receive. And, in the Republican party, if a candidate wins enough write-in votes in a winner-take-all primary, he or she can win all of that state's delegates to the convention.

The Democratic party rules require that state Democratic parties must "take all feasible steps to restrict participation in the delegate selection process to Democratic voters only." The purpose of this rule is to prevent what is called "crossover voting." A crossover vote is when a person who is registered as a member of one party, crosses over in the primary to vote for a Presidential candidate in the other party. The Democrats have attempted to prohibit crossover voting but have allowed it to continue in Michigan and Wisconsin. However, it is expected eventually to be eliminated in those states. The Republican party leaves the question of crossover voting up to the state Republican parties or state law.

The national political parties are in a unique position regarding the setting of rules for the selection of delegates to their Presidential conventions. The Supreme Court, in the

"ENTERING ALL THESE PRIMARIES IS REALLY EXHILARATING. TODAY I SEE I'M SCHEDULED TO MEET WITH SOME LEADING CITIZENS, DISCUSS THEIR PROBLEMS, AND TRY TO FIND SOME SOLUTIONS. WHERE ARE WE?"

case of *Cousins* v. *Wigoda* (1975), ruled that national parties can establish their own rules for the selection of delegates to their national conventions, *even if the rules conflict with state laws.*

The Democrats have taken their responsibility to expand the nominating process in their party seriously. To encourage full participation of all Democrats in the process, they insist that all state Democratic parties adopt "affirmative action" programs. The goal of these programs is to encourage full participation of all Democrats, not only in the nominating process but in all activities and organizations of the party. To see that such affirmative action programs are enacted, the Democratic party also created a Compliance Review Commission, consisting of twenty-five members. The CRC was instructed to review all state affirmative action programs and recommend changes in these programs to bring them into compliance with party rules.

The Republicans, on the other hand, have not moved as forcefully to broaden participation in their party affairs. They do have "positive action" programs to achieve this goal. But they put it on a voluntary basis and have no provisions for enforcing the programs.

Of course, the nomination process is constantly undergoing change and, in fact, additional reforms are still being studied. At the 1976 convention, the party created the Winograd Commission to study ways of improving the primary system. And as this book went to press, the commission was considering shortening the primary period to thirteen weeks —from the second Tuesday in March to the second Tuesday in June. It was also considering ways of making victories in the later primaries count for more than victories in the early primaries.

Despite the different approaches of the two parties to nominating convention delegates and the diversities in the state laws and regulations, primary campaigns have come to play an important and critical role in the American political process. Candidates make a special effort to do well in the early primaries, thereby giving a "bandwagon" effect to their campaign and demonstrating that they have voter appeal outside their home state. This is one reason why the New Hampshire primary plays such an important role in the primary campaign. By state law, the New Hampshire primary must be the first primary held in the election year. A few years ago, the New Hampshire primary was in March. But to remain first it has been moved to February 24. And it will continue to move its date forward if necessary to remain first, even if, as one state legislator put it, "it is necessary to hold it at halftime of the Super Bowl [January 1]."

Long before any of the candidates have "filed" (which means notifying the authorities that they intend to run) for the New Hampshire primary, the press and the politicians begin to speculate as to how well the "front-runner" must do in New Hampshire to maintain a good position. The "front-runner" of course, is the leading contender at any given moment. For example, an incumbent President who is seeking reelection is automatically the "front-runner" in his party.

Because New Hampshire is the first primary, it is the first time a party's front-runner is challenged by another member of the same party. Or, if there is no front-runner, it is the first time the candidates have a chance to show their voting strength at the polls. And in the case of a candidate challenging the front-runner (especially an incumbent President), it is possible for the press and the politicians to say candidates score a "victory" in a primary, even if they actually lose it. Senator Eugene McCarthy was said to have scored a "victory" in the 1968 New Hampshire primary, even though President Johnson (who was a write-in candidate) received more votes. Johnson, it was said, should have defeated McCarthy by a bigger margin. And in 1972, Senator

George McGovern, running in the New Hampshire Democratic primary against Senator Edmund Muskie, actually was credited with a substantial "victory" even though he received fewer votes than Muskie. It was said that because New Hampshire was next to Senator Muskie's home state of Maine, he had to receive at least 50 percent of the vote to be the "winner." Actually, he won the primary with 46.4 percent of the vote, but it was considered a "defeat." Contrast this with the 1972 Florida Democratic primary. It was conceded that the South's strongest vote getter, George Wallace, would probably win. And he did, with only 42 percent of the vote, compared to Muskie's 47 percent in New Hampshire the previous month. But Wallace's Florida win was interpreted as a "tremendous victory."

The truth is that interpreting the results of a primary is often very complicated. Also, in many states the total vote is small and the population is not really typical of the country as a whole. Thus, the vote is almost meaningless, except for the psychological factor and what politicians and the press say about the results. New Hampshire, for example, is 99 percent white and 39 percent Republican (which is unusually high when you consider that only 18 percent of the voters, nationally, consider themselves Republican). And in 1976, only 60 percent of the 142,655 people eligible to vote in the New Hampshire primary turned out. Yet the New Hampshire Democratic primary, in almost every election year since 1952, has played an important role in the nomination of the Democratic Presidential candidate.

Of course, the primary elections in the larger states are even more important. Not only are the big state results analyzed carefully (and, even so, may be interpreted incorrectly: New York, for example, has one of the most politically complicated primary structures in the country), but there are a large number of delegate votes at stake. In the

1976 New York primary, there were 274 Democratic and 154 Republican delegates chosen for the convention; in Pennsylvania, 178 Democratic and 103 Republican; in Michigan, 133 Democratic and 84 Republican.

The tension and excitement builds up in the campaign to the last primaries on June 8—in New Jersey, Ohio, and California. Politicians call these the "World Series," or the "Super Bowl," of the primary campaign because there are a total of 540 Democratic and 331 Republican delegates sent to the conventions from the last three primaries.

There have been many historically important primaries in recent years: John F. Kennedy's victory over Hubert Humphrey in West Virginia in 1960 was considered important because it demonstrated that a Catholic candidate could do well in a Protestant state. George McGovern's victory over Hubert Humphrey in California in 1972 and Barry Goldwater's victory over Nelson Rockefeller in California in 1964 were both considered crushing blows to the losers, coming right on the eve of the national conventions. And Jimmy Carter's victory in Pennsylvania, with its heavy labor vote, was considered by many the turning point for Carter in the 1976 primaries.

With all its faults, most students of politics agree that the primary campaigns today serve an important function in weeding out candidates who really are not "Presidential timber." By the time the candidates stagger exhausted into their respective conventions, the party members and the American voters have a pretty good idea who the serious candidates are. In fact, the lesser candidates have usually dropped out of the race by the time of the national conventions.

In 1976, approximately 75 percent of the delegates to the conventions were chosen in primary elections. Some 29 million people voted in the primaries (18.1 million in the

Democratic primaries and 10.8 million in the Republican). This is compared to 22.2 million voting in the primaries in 1972. Perhaps the most significant thing that can be said about the primaries is that President Jimmy Carter was nominated by the primary election process, and it was probably one of the fairest and most broadly representative nominations in American political history.

CHAPTER

4

FINANCING THE CAMPAIGNS AND NATIONAL CONVENTIONS

One of the basic principles of the American political system is that it should be financed by contributions from average citizens who expect nothing in return but good, honest government. However, it has not always been easy or possible to persuade people to contribute the money needed to finance political parties and the campaigns of their candidates. At the same time, through the years, the cost of financing political campaigns has increased dramatically. In the 1976 primary campaign alone, Jimmy Carter spent $11.4 million; Gerald Ford spent $13.5 million.

In recent years, with costs increasing and the average citizen showing varying degrees of enthusiasm for contributing money to political campigns, the candidates and their parties have had to turn more and more to special fund-raising methods. They have used such techniques as direct mail campaigns, telephone requests, and fund-raising dinners. Sometimes the candidates themselves have contributed large sums out of their personal funds, which is considered bad because it gives special advantages and rewards to the rich.

However, even these sources have not been enough to finance the modern political campaign. The cost of television, newspaper, and radio advertising is increasing, and all are considered essential. In addition, money is needed to pay for professional members of the staff, travel, telephones, and other necessities of a political campaign.

As a result, more and more candidates have had to rely on special interest groups for their money—usually big industries and big labor unions.

Both political parties accept money from either group, and both groups contribute to both parties. But it is generally agreed that the Democratic party is most heavily financed by big labor and the Republican party by big business.

Candidates from both parties, of course, continue to try to raise money from private citizens. And they usually stress in their campaign literature how much money they received from private citizens and how this demonstrates their popular support. But most of the money continues to come from special interest groups, who usually expect something in return. They want laws that favor their organizations, or, at the very least, they want "access" to the President. Consequently, a movement has developed to reform the methods for financing our political campaigns, including the primary campaigns.

The movement actually began before the Watergate scandals. But during that time, it became evident that President Nixon's supporters were carrying the corruption of political financing one step further than the granting of political favors for financial contributions. Nixon's fundraisers put pressure on potential contributors, threatening to use the power of government *against* them if they did not contribute.

The increasing corruption in the financing of campaigns, combined with the increasing cost of campaigning, finally led to a new set of campaign financing laws. The most important features of the new laws:

★ made Federal funds available to Presidential candidates, including funds for primary campaigns;
★ limited the amount of money that a candidate who accepts Federal funds can spend on a campaign;
★ limited the amount of money people and organizations could contribute to campaigns;
★ strengthened the rules for reporting how much money was raised and from whom, and how much money was spent and on what;
★ created an organization for enforcing the laws;
★ provided each party with funds for its national conventions.

"IT'S ALL JUNK MAIL. IT'S FROM CANDIDATES
WHO WANT CAMPAIGN CONTRIBUTIONS."

Federal Funds for Primaries: A candidate for President wanting to qualify for federal campaign funds may spend no more than $20 million on the Presidential campaign and $10 million on the campaign to win the nomination of his or her party. However, if the candidate does not wish to receive federal funds, there is no limit to how much may be spent on either the primary campaign or the general election.

Federal Funds for General Elections: To qualify for federal funds in a primary campaign, a candidate must raise at least $5,000 in each of 20 states in amounts of no more than $250 per contribution. If this is done, the government will match funds for the primary campaign up to a total of $5 million. A major party is entitled to $20 million to wage a Presidential campaign. The party and the candidate do not have to raise funds to qualify for this money. Minor party candidates are also entitled to federal funds. However, they do not receive their money until after the election and then the amount depends on the number of popular votes they received.

Personal Funds: Candidates who accept federal funds can only use $50,000 in family or personal funds in the campaign.

Limits on Contributions: Individuals can contribute a maximum of $1,000 to any candidate during an election. The primary campaign counts as one election, which means that an individual could contribute another $1,000 in the general election to that candidate if he or she wins the nomination.

It is illegal for industries to give money directly to political candidates or parties. However, industries have gotten

"LET'S FACE IT—IF HE USES ALL THE EQUAL TIME HE'S ENTITLED TO, HE'S BOUND TO MAKE A FOOL OF HIMSELF."

around this by contributing money through their corporate executives or sometimes secretly. Labor unions have not been prohibited from giving money to political campaigns, and their funds are usually given through what are called political action committees. Wealthy individuals have also given large amounts of money to Presidential campaigns in the past, often in the hopes of being awarded an ambassadorship. Under the new laws, which are very complicated, the amount of money that private individuals and special interest groups can contribute to a campaign are restricted. However, it is still possible for large amounts of money to find their way to Presidential candidates from private sources. An individual donor, for example, can give up to $25,000 to a political party, with the understanding that the money be spread around among a number of campaigns. And the Supreme Court has ruled that there is no limit on how much a private individual or special interest group can spend on behalf of a Presidential candidate—so long as the money is spent separately and independently and not coordinated with or considered part of the Presidential or primary campaign.

Enforcing the Laws: The new laws establish a Federal Election Commission empowered to enforce the laws. There are also strict regulations governing the disclosure of the source of a candidate's money and how it is spent.

Federal Funds for National Conventions: The new election law provides $2 million to each major political party to finance its national convention. In the past, the conventions have been financed by general party funds and special funds, such as money from the city in which the convention was being held and advertising sold in the special convention programs.

The 1976 Presidental election was the first in which the new laws were in effect. The impact of these laws on the campaign financing issue are still being studied, and the results may well lead to further changes in the law, when the students of government and the courts determine how well the current laws are working.

CHAPTER

5

THE PRESIDENTIAL NOMINATING CONVENTIONS

It is difficult to say which is preferable—watching a convention on television or attending it in person. It is certainly more exciting to attend in person, especially if you have a pass that permits you to go down to the convention floor. On the other hand, television coverage of the conventions has now become so expert and extensive that you see far more viewing it on television than you do when you attend. The truth is, there is so much going on at a convention and in so many different places, that no one person can keep track of it all. The TV networks use several television reporters and mini-camera teams who relay what is happening back to the newscasters in their booths high above the convention floor. The newscasters and the program directors select what is the most important or interesting or colorful and relay it to the millions of televiewers across the nation. This is why most people attending a convention always keep in touch with a television set in one of the many conference rooms and lounges in the convention hall.

Many months in advance of the convention, the party's National Committee will begin to consider the various cities that might host the convention. Because the conventions bring prestige and business to a city, city officials around the country compete for the conventions by offering the parties payments in the form of cash and services if the committee will choose their city. The committee, in turn, must consider a number of factors: Does the city have enough hotel space and a suitable auditorium to handle not only the delegates and the politicians but all the television equipment and thousands of reporters who want to attend the conventions? Also, is there sufficient transportation around town, good restaurants, and airport and railroad facilities? Finally, there are political considerations: If the city is in the home state of one of the leading candidates, all the other candidates would object. Also, a party usually likes to hold its convention in a city and state in which the mayor and gov-

"WE GET THIS ONE FOR UNDERSTANDING HOW THE DEMOCRATIC NOMINATION SYSTEM WORKS."

ernor are members of that party. During the 1976 campaign, one of the principal reasons the Democrats picked New York City was to demonstrate their support for a city that was having financial problems and that for many years had supported the Democratic party.

The conventions have four functions: To nominate the Presidential and Vice-Presidential candidates; to write the party platform; to establish the rules of the convention; and to issue the "Call" of the convention, which authorizes the National Committee to hold another convention in four years.

Much of the work of the convention is done by committees, which meet off the convention floor in conference rooms. They report the results of their work to the convention, usually on the last day, and the delegates vote their approval or disapproval of the committee's work.

The convention is called to order under the temporary chairmanship of the chairman of the party's National Committee. On the first day, he or she takes care of the routine business, which traditionally includes brief addresses by such people as the governor of the state in which the convention is held and the mayor of the host city (if those officials are members of that party), the convention manager, the party's finance chairman, the treasurer, and the National Chairman of the party. The chairman then turns the convention over to another temporary chairman, who has been designated as the "keynote speaker." If things go on schedule, this happens just about the time the television networks go into "prime time" in the evenings, to assure the largest possible television audience for the keynote speaker.

At this point, it is important to explain the role of the party's National Committee and the part it and its chairman play in organizing a convention. Each party has a National Committee made up of one man and one woman from each state, plus the District of Columbia, Guam, Puerto Rico, and the Virgin Islands. The committees meet from time to time to conduct party business, the most important of which is the election of the National Chairman. This person is usually handpicked by the Presidential nominee of the convention or the President, if that party holds the White House. However, if a party suffers a defeat in a Presidential election, there is often a fight for chairmanship of the party afterward.

The chairmanship of a political party is a very powerful position, especially in the "out party," meaning the party that does not control the White House. The chairman has an office in Washington and a large headquarters staff. One of the difficult problems facing the chairman and his or her staff is maintaining a strict neutrality during the Presidential primary campaigns and in preparing for the convention, which is the chairman's responsibility. The committee is expected to support for President any member of the party that wins the nomination, and this is not always easy. The chairman and the staff naturally have personal favorites. At the same time, all the competing candidates are watching the chairman and the committee staff very, very closely for any sign of favoritism toward any of the other candidates. Hence, all preparations the National Committee makes for the convention, such as picking the city for the convention, deciding the number of people that will attend the convention from each state, allocating space to the candidates and their staffs, and picking the temporary and permanent convention chairmen, must have the full approval of all the leading contenders for the nomination.

One of the temporary chairmen—the "keynote speaker" —is usually an up-and-coming young party member who is a forceful speaker and a dedicated party partisan. He or she is called upon to sound the "keynote" of the convention—that is, to summarize dramatically all the reasons why the party will be organizing its efforts in the months ahead to either maintain control of the White House (if the party is "in") or "throw the rascals out" (if the party is "out"). The keynote speaker is usually careful to avoid any indication of preference for the Presidential nominee (unless that has already been determined) and stresses the fact that however divided the party might be right now (over the question of picking a candidate), once the choice is made, it will leave the convention hall united as never before to take up the job at hand, which is defeating the opposition. The keynote speech usually concludes the first day's activities.

On the second day, the first order of business is usually the approval of the Credentials Committee Report, and in the past this has often produced the first real fight at the convention. As Senator Alan Cranston, chairman of the Credentials Committee at the 1976 Democratic Convention, said in his opening remarks: "At the very first Democratic Convention in 1832, the first Report of the Credentials Committee was rendered—and the first convention floor fight was waged."

Essentially, what the fights are over is whether a state delegation at the convention (usually supporting one particular candidate) is the official, authorized delegation, or whether another delegation (usually supporting another candidate) might be the authorized one. Down through the years, in both parties, there have been some historic fights over convention credentials. At the 1952 Republican Convention, there was a famous fight over seating the Texas delegation, which was very critical to winning the nomination for Dwight D. Eisenhower. Another credentials fight occurred at the 1972 Democratic Convention over the seating of the California delegation. It involved 151 delegates. The McGovern forces successfully fought off the challenges to the California delegation, which supported him.

There were, in fact, so many credentials challenges at the 1972 Democratic Convention that the fight went on until three in the morning, seriously disrupting the convention schedule and driving the television audience to other channels not carrying the convention. This led to the efforts of the Democratic party to reform its method of selecting and certifying delegates to the convention. In 1976, there were only 50 delegate challenges involving 207 delegates (compared to 118 challenges in 1972 involving 2,289 delegates), and all of those were settled in the Compliance Review Commission, rather than on the convention floor. So, in the Democratic party, at least, the tiresome and lengthy floor fights over delegate credentials may be a thing of the past. However, the Republican party has not adopted similar reforms, so future Republican conventions may still be marred by credentials fights.

After the approval of the credentials, the convention is usually turned over to the permanent chairman. In recent years, Speakers and former Speakers of the House of Representatives have been the usual choice for permanent chairman, primarily because of the need for a good parliamentarian who can maintain order in a large meeting. A Presidential convention is governed by a set of parliamentary rules very much like those that govern Congress or a state legislature. The chairman calls the meeting to order, tells the sergeant at arms to clear the aisles, and then the convention gets down to its serious business.

THE PLATFORM

Before the convention starts to nominate its Presidential candidate, it must vote on and adopt the many "planks" in the party "platform." The party platform traditionally is the collection of promises and ideals it intends to "stand on" in

"THE CONVENTION IS EVEN MORE WIDE OPEN
THAN WE EXPECTED IT TO BE."

the Presidential election. It presents, in printed form, the things the party and its candidates will promise to do, or try to do, if they are elected.

Usually the platforms are worked out before the convention. There are two different approaches to writing the party platform, depending on whether the party controls the White House. If the party controls the White House, the platform is usually written under close supervision of the President's staff and submitted to the convention for approval. Little opposition is expected to this platform as long as the President is popular within the party and has control over it. If the President has opposition within the party, there very likely could be a fight over the platform at the convention.

On the other hand, if the party does not control the White House, the National Committee organizes the platform-writing committee in such a way that all the special groups have a voice in writing the platform. This includes representatives, or the supporters of, all the leading Presidential candidates in the party.

In 1976, the Democratic party went further than either party has ever gone in opening up the writing of the platform to all members of the party. Its Platform Committee, under the chairmanship of Governor Wendell Anderson of Minnesota, consisted of 150 members and it held four regional meetings around the country and a four-day meeting in Washington, two months before the convention. A total of 500 witnesses testified before the committee, giving their views on what the platform should contain. Then it was presented at the convention and adopted virtually without a fight.

One reason the platform went through so smoothly, in contrast to the 1968 and 1972 Democratic conventions when there were major fights over the platform, was the reforms adoped by the party after the 1972 convention. At that time it was possible to bring a minority report (one opposed to the majority report) of the Platform Committee to the floor of the convention if only 10 percent of the Platform Committee voted to do so. But after the 1972 convention, the Democrats decided that the place to fight over the platform was in the Platform Committee and not on the floor of the convention in front of the television audience. So they decreed that 25 percent of the members of the Platform Committee must agree before a minority report could be brought to the floor of the convention for a vote.

Politicians and reporters always watch the voting on certain platform planks as an indication of how much strength the Presidential candidates have at the convention. If a leading candidate is known to favor a plank and another leading contender is known to oppose it, when it comes to the floor for a vote, you can measure the depth of a candidate's support by the way the voting goes. The most dramatic example of the platform as a barometer of convention sentiment occurred in 1964 at the Republican convention. The two leading contenders for the nomination were the conservative Senator Barry Goldwater of Arizona and the more liberal Governor Nelson Rockefeller of New York. The Platform Committee, which was conservative, adopted a platform acceptable to Barry Goldwater. Rockefeller's people attempted to change the platform on the floor of the convention by offering amendments. However, on each vote they were defeated by Goldwater supporters, and the wise politicians and political reporters said, "The convention is over—Goldwater has the nomination"—which was the way it turned out.

When the party platform is finally adopted, it is usually forgotten—except by the opposing candidates who look for opportunities to point out where the Presidential candidate does not support his or her own party's platform.

NOMINATING THE PRESIDENTIAL CANDIDATE

With the platform adopted, the convention can then settle down to its most important function—picking the party's Presidential candidate. In both parties, this occurs when any candidate wins a majority of the votes of all the official delegates certified to attend the convention. Each party has a slightly different method for determining how many delegates can participate in a convention and each allows a different number. In 1976, there were 2,258 delegates to the Republican convention in Kansas City and 3,048 delegates to the Democratic convention in New York, who were allowed only 3,008 votes because the Democrats permit fractional voting. Hence, victory for Jimmy Carter meant winning 1,505 votes and victory for Gerald Ford meant winning 1,130 votes.

The method for determining just how many delegates will attend a convention—and the number varies every four years—is complicated. But in both parties, the guiding formula is the population of a state and the voting strength of the party in that state. Thus, the number of delegates a state is allocated is usually based on the number of Senators and Representatives that state has in Congress plus a "bonus" of delegates for any state in which the party has done well in recent elections for governor, Congress, and the Presidency.

Any state party that works hard and wins victories at the polls is rewarded by additional voting strength at the Presidential nominating convention.

The nominating procedure works this way: The permanent chairman announces the roll call of the convention "for the purpose of nominating the next President of the United States." It is the custom to follow alphabetical order in calling the roll of states, with Alabama always being called first, and Wyoming last.

The usual practice is for the first state called to either place a candidate in nomination or yield to another state for the purpose of placing a candidate in nomination. At that point, the chairman of the state delegation announces to the chairman that a member of that delegation is coming to the podium for the purpose of placing a candidate in nomination. There is much wild cheering and demonstrating before the chairman manages to bring the convention to order for the purpose of hearing the nomination speech. This is usually given by one of the candidate's better-known supporters. The speaker praises the candidate, gives a brief flowery biography, reciting the nominee's public record, and then advances all the arguments for nominating the candidate. There are also a series of seconding speeches by people from different walks of political life designed to demonstrate widespread support for the nominee. However, before the seconding speeches comes one of the great traditions of the conventions, the demonstration—wild pandemonium, with frenzied men and women of all ages dancing around the aisles carrying placards and signs, sometimes accompanied by small marching bands, all designed to show unbridled enthusiasm for the candidate whose name was just placed in nomination.

There was a time when these demonstrations were quite sincere and they would often last for hours. The purpose was, literally, to stampede the convention into accepting a particular candidate. As time went on, though, the demonstrations became more and more controlled, until they were virtually organized by professional demonstrators. Then came television and the awareness by convention officials that the television viewers could only take so much of a demonstration and so many seconding speeches before they turned to another channel or turned the set off.

So the parties moved to control the demonstrations. The Democrats now limit the total time for placing a person

"WELL, I FOUND IT EASIER TO MAKE UP
MY MIND ON THE VICE-PRESIDENTIAL
CANDIDATES AND I'LL VOTE ACCORDINGLY."

in nomination—including the seconding speeches and the demonstration—to fifteen minutes. The Republicans limit the speeches to fifteen minutes, but do not restrict the planned demonstrations. In neither case are the time limits strictly observed.

The nominating process continues until every candidate has been nominated. And this often includes many candidates who are not serious nominees known as "favorite sons." A favorite son is a very popular politician in a state, usually the governor or a senator, whom the state party wants to honor and give some national television exposure, either to help in the favorite son's own reelection that fall or perhaps to start the favorite son on a Presidential campaign four years later. However, "favorite son" nominations often have an even more practical motive: A state delegation may want to remain uncommitted in the balloting until it has an indication of who is going to win. So it votes for a "favorite son." Then it can get on the "bandwagon" later and cast its votes for the winner without ever having cast its votes for the winner's opponent.

Again, because of television, convention officials have had to control the favorite-son nominations. Too many were being made just to get the television spotlight and it began to bore the viewers. Now, in both parties, a candidate for nomination has to have serious support from at least three states before the name can be placed in nomination.

After all the nominations are made, the balloting for the Presidential nomination begins. At this point the chairman of the convention will call the name of a state, and the chairman of that state delegation will say something like, "The great state of Colorado, home of the Grand Canyon, casts seventeen votes for John Doe, twelve votes for Jane Smith, and eight votes for Robert Brown," or "The great state of Minnesota casts all of its sixty-five votes for the next President of the United States, John Brown."

At one time, the Democrat convention operated under the "unit rule," which meant that if a majority of delegates in a state delegation were for one candidate, then the delegation would vote as a unit, casting all of its votes for that candidate. However, Republicans have not permitted the unit rule in modern times and neither have the Democrats since 1968. In both parties today, the votes are cast individually for any candidate a delegate prefers, and if there is any question about the vote, anyone in the delegation may call for a poll of the delegation. This takes time and is usually annoying to the television audience. But because it is so critical to the democratization of the conventions, it is unlikely that delegation polling will ever be eliminated.

The politicians and political reporters at a convention can usually tell about halfway through the voting whether a candidate has enough votes to make it on the first ballot, or whether the nomination might take more than one ballot. Historically, there have been many Presidential nominations that were made only after several ballots. In 1924, in New York, the Democrats took 103 ballots to nominate John W. Davis.

However, not since 1952 has either party had to take more than one ballot to nominate its candidate. But many Democrats feel that the new rules governing the selection of delegates will make it harder for any candidate to come into the convention with enough votes to win on the first ballot. In fact, many political observers thought this would be the case in 1976 and that it would lead to what the politicians call a "brokered convention." This means that the political bosses get together in "smoke-filled rooms" (which are not so smoke-filled today because fewer politicians smoke) and make deals. A typical deal would be that one candidate might offer another candidate the Vice-Presidency or an important post in the Cabinet in return for that candidate's support and votes. At the Republican convention in 1940, Governor Thomas E. Dewey was ahead on the first ballot with 360 votes over 189 for Senator Robert Taft and 105 for Wendell Willkie. Dewey offered Senator Arthur Vandenburg the Vice-Presidency for his support, but, Vandenburg wrote in his diary, "I offered to flip a coin with Dewey to see which side of the ticket each would take." But Dewey held out for the Presidential nomination, until it eventually went to Willkie, who picked Senator Charles McNary as his Vice-Presidential running mate.

In both parties today, the way delegates vote on the first ballot is governed by a strict set of rules set down either by state law or party rules. This is called "binding." And it varies from state to state and in both parties. For example, in some states the results of the primary or the party caucus is binding for only one ballot, meaning the delegates *must* vote the way they were instructed to by the primary results or by the state convention. But after the first ballot, they are free to vote for anyone they want. In other states, delegates are bound for two ballots, and others for three. And in a few states, the delegates are bound on all ballots, until they are released by the candidates to whom they are pledged. But it is felt that at any convention in the future, if a candidate does not win on the first ballot, the convention will probably break wide open and the traditional wheeling and dealing for the nomination will take place.

On the second and third ballots, it usually becomes apparent which candidates have the most strength. Delegates will begin to drop away from the weaker candidates and the "favorite sons," and the state delegations will start to bargain for votes. There are telephone connections between all the state delegations on the floor and the campaign headquarters of the various candidates. A typical "deal" might be something like promising a farm state a voice in naming the Secretary of Agriculture if that state will cast all its votes for a certain candidate. And, of course, all states at this point want to be with the winner, and every state would like to be the state that puts the winning candidate over the top.

Eventually, one nominee emerges who has the confidence of the majority of delegates—or has been able to negotiate and bargain for enough votes. When the word is out that one state is going to switch its ballot and swing its vote to one of the leading candidates—enough to secure the nomination—the convention hall is gripped with excitement. You can feel it, like electricity, in the air. Then, when the state makes it official, there is real pandemonium, even greater than when the candidates were placed in nomination.

When it is all over, there is then the question of whether the winner will appear on the floor that night, or decide not to appear at the convention until it is time to make the acceptance speech the next night. Often, especially in the case of an incumbent President, the candidate may not even be in the city. The convention work is done by the campaign manager, although the nominee is in constant touch by telephone. The trend in recent years, however, has been for the winning candidate and his family to appear in person the night of the nomination, at least for a brief wave to the convention.

Having finally received the Presidential nomination, after perhaps as long as two years of campaigning, totally exhausted and with a campaign staff in a state of frenzy and perhaps even in confusion, the nominee must then make the first—and sometimes most important—decision as a candidate for President. The nominee must pick a Vice-Presidential candidate or determine how the Vice-Presidential candidate will be nominated.

PICKING THE VICE-PRESIDENTIAL CANDIDATE

The office of Vice-President of the United States is one of the most peculiar positions in our government. Woodrow Wilson, who later became President, was a scholar at Princeton when he wrote a famous study of American politics in which he said: "There is very little to be said about the Vice-President. . . . His importance consists in the fact that he may cease to be Vice-President."

In other words, historically, the office has had no importance except that someday the Vice-President might have to become President, if the President dies in office or is forced to resign. Few Vice-Presidents have been remembered in history, unless they went on to become President. And few politicians have ever sought the office. The one exception was James K. Polk, the only man in American political history to go into a convention as an avowed candidate for Vice-President. Polk has another distinction: He is history's original "dark horse" candidate. At the Democratic convention of 1844, the overwhelming favorite was Martin Van Buren. But when he let it be known that he was opposed to the annexation of Texas, the convention turned against him. But it could not agree on an alternative. Polk, a Congressman, former governor of Tennessee, and a candidate for the Vice-Presidency, was virtually unknown—a "dark horse." He was finally placed in nomination on the eighth ballot, and received only forty-four votes. However, Polk favored the annexation of Texas, and he suddenly seemed a perfect compromise. With former President Andrew Jackson's support, he was nominated on the next ballot. As his Vice-Presidential running mate, the convention picked Pennsylvania Senator George M. Dallas, who is remembered only because the city of Dallas was named after him.

Dallas also is significant in the evolution of the office of the Vice-President because it was there, on November 22,

1963, that John F. Kennedy was assassinated and Vice-President Lyndon Johnson abruptly became President of the United States. This tragedy, which is still affecting American politics, served to remind the American people that, although the duties of the Vice-President as defined in the Constitution are minimal, the choice of the Vice-Presidential candidate is one of the most important acts of the convention.

This should have come as no surprise to the American people. Before Kennedy, Presidents William Henry Harrison, Zachary Taylor, Abraham Lincoln, James A. Garfield, William McKinley, Warren G. Harding, and Franklin D. Roosevelt had all died in office, abruptly making Presidents of Vice-Presidents John Tyler, Millard Fillmore, Andrew Johnson, Chester A. Arthur, Theodore Roosevelt, Calvin Coolidge, and Harry S. Truman, respectively. The death of Kennedy and the resignation of Richard Nixon, which elevated Vice-President Gerald Ford to the Presidency, served to further emphasize the fact that the Vice-Presidency is now a very critical office in the government. In fact, the office has become so important that it can become an issue itself in a campaign. The voters now look very critically at a Presidential candidate's choice of a running mate and, if the choice does not meet with their approval, it can seriously affect the candidate's chances of being elected. In 1972, Presidential candidate George McGovern was forced to drop his Vice-Presidential choice, Senator Thomas Eagleton of Missouri, from the ticket when it was revealed that Senator Eagleton had had psychiatric problems earlier in his career.

Thus, the Vice-Presidential candidate must be a person who has the qualities necessary for leadership, as well as being close politically and temperamentally to the President. As former Vice-President Hubert Humphrey once said, "The Vice-President will be and is what the President wants him to be . . . a loyal, faithful friend and servant."

The Vice-President's only duty under the Constitution is

to preside over the Senate of the United States and cast a vote in the Senate if there is a tie in the voting. And even this vote in the Senate, which is exercised very rarely, will most likely be as the President orders.

Technically, the Vice-Presidential nominee of a party is picked at the convention in the same manner as the Presidential candidate. There are nominations from the floor of the convention and seconding speeches and demonstrations. But the effect is not the same, because the Presidential candidate has already let it be known who the Vice-Presidential choice is.

However, at the Democratic convention in 1956, Presidential nominee Adlai Stevenson did allow the convention to pick a candidate, without naming his own choice. The convention choice was Senator Estes Kefauver of Tennessee, although young Senator Jack Kennedy of Massachusetts launched such an impressive and dramatic campaign for the Vice-Presidency at the convention that he was clearly the choice of the television audience. (It was also Kennedy's first exposure to a national audience and it helped to start him on the way to the Presidential nomination in 1960.)

Historically, the choice of Vice-Presidential candidates are made with two main thoughts in mind: to unite the party, and to help elect the President. These factors are still foremost in the minds of the Presidential nominee when picking a candidate at the convention. If the party is divided on a controversial issue, it usually happens that the most powerful elements in the party at the convention will reflect the sentiment of the party by nominating a Presidential candidate whose position on that issue is similar to the position taken by the majority of the people in the party. Then, the Presidential nominee will try to "unite" the party by urging the convention to pick as Vice-President a person who took the other side of the issue dividing the party.

However, if the Presidential nominee is picked as a

moderate between the liberals and the conservatives, neither a liberal nor a conservative can be picked as a running mate without "unbalancing" the ticket. Thus, Richard Nixon, a compromise candidate between the liberals and the conservatives at the 1968 Republican convention, picked Maryland Governor Spiro Agnew as his running mate. At that time, very little was known about Agnew, and he—like Nixon—was acceptable to both the liberals and the conservatives in the party.

Another factor that has historically influenced the choice of a running mate is the geographical consideration. It is thought desirable to balance an Easterner with a Westerner or a Southerner or a Midwesterner—and vice versa. Because the South has been so important to the Democratic party since the Civil War, Democratic conventions usually have ended up with a northern or eastern liberal Presidential candidate and a southern, more conservative, Vice-Presidential candidate. And many people have pointed out that, considering the growing importance of the New South, or sunbelt, in the country, it is not surprising that the Democrats reversed this tradition in 1976 and picked a southern conservative Presidential candidate and a northern liberal Vice-Presidential candidate—Walter Mondale of Minnesota.

Ultimately, of course, it is the responsibility of the convention to decide who the Vice-Presidential candidate is. And it could rebel against the choice of the Presidential nominee. But this is unlikely to happen. In the first place, most members of a party that has gathered to pick their Presidential candidate are very much aware of the need for unity in the election coming up. And they are aware that the opposition and the voters are always watching carefully for signs of dissention, which in politics is taken as a sign of weakness. More important, once someone wins the party's

Presidential nomination, that person is truly the leader of that party and its most powerful member. Some day the candidate might be President of the United States, and most members of the party do not want to alienate the President of the United States. As everyone in public life is aware, it always helps to have a friend in the White House.

When the formality of nominating the Vice-Presidential candidate is completed, the Vice-Presidential nominee gives an acceptance speech. This is followed by the closing event of the convention (usually planned for prime television time)—the acceptance speech of the Presidential candidate. In it the candidate accepts the nomination and promises, with the help of the party, to lead them to victory in November.

The speech is usually followed by some demonstration of unity. Leaders of all factions of the party—including some who might have opposed the Presidential candidate during the primaries—are invited to the platform. They usually clasp hands with the Presidential candidate and raise them in a victory signal. All this is designed to assure all members of the party—and the millions of voters in the television audience—that the party is united as never before.

When the convention is over, the new candidates, their families, and all the leaders in the party usually retire to vacation retreats all over the country for a few weeks of well-deserved rest, which they are going to need. Soon they will be campaigning all over again in the general election, which lasts from Labor Day until the second Tuesday in November every four years.

It is interesting to remember that the Olympics and the American Presidential elections occur every four years, and in the same years. And it would be hard to say which is the more strenuous event.

CHAPTER 6

CONCLUSION

The two most important factors in making America a great nation are its geographic location and natural resources (which helped create our wealth and security) and its political system (which helped assure our freedom). And one of the reasons the political system is so great is that it is flexible enough to accommodate changing conditions.

The Constitution says nothing about political parties. But it did create a political system that allowed political parties to develop. It also created a system of laws, which govern the men and women who operate our political institutions, as well as the institutions themselves. And the advantage of a government of laws is that you can change a bad law. But without law and political freedom, it is very difficult to get rid of a bad leader.

The system of primaries, caucuses, and conventions for nominating our political leaders has evolved over the years within the framework of the Constitutional guidelines. It is a continually changing process, reflecting the changing mood and conditions of the country, as well as the concern of citizens who have sought to improve the system by encouraging broader participation in it.

The desire to create a system in which the people had a voice in nominating the candidates led to the primary system. In 1976, there were thirty-one primaries, and, it might be asked, if thirty-one primaries are a good thing, why don't we have fifty primaries? The truth is that even with thirty-one primaries, the students of government are beginning to have doubts about the primary system. They say that primaries are too expensive, both for the candidates and the states. In the 1976 Presidential campaign, $16.5 million was spent by the candidates before January 1, 1976 (when the primary campaigns began), and $72 million was spent by the candidates in the campaigns. It cost the states at least $22.6 million to administer the primaries. This figure is con-

"HE WAS AN ALTERNATE DELEGATE WHO NEVER GOT A CHANCE TO SAY ANYTHING ABOUT ANYTHING."

sidered low, but the data are not available for accurately determining the costs.

It is also felt that even thirty-one primaries are physically exhausting to the candidates, which threatens their health and forces candidates to neglect their jobs. It is also argued by the party professionals that the primary system, combined with the power of television, is decreasing the power of the political party and making it increasingly possible for a demagogue to win the nomination without the support of a party. They argue that an organized, effective political party is not only a healthy thing for the country and the states but necessary to win a general election. Finally, it is said that the system is too complicated and confusing. As one study of the 1976 primary campaigns prepared for the Democratic National Committee pointed out, "The outcome of last year's primaries was, in many cases, determined by the knowledge or ignorance of the many quirks in the individual election laws."

This kind of criticism has prompted reformers to continue to look for ways to improve the system. There have been, for example, proposals to create a national primary, or at least a series of regional primaries and to simplify the state primaries and make them more uniform from state to state. And, of course, there are continuing efforts to broaden participation in the primaries by making the affirmative action programs in every state more effective.

Questions have also been raised about the role of the conventions. Increasingly, the conventions have done little more than ratify the results of the primary campaigns. Only once, since 1952, has a convention done anything more than nominate the winner of the key primaries. That was in 1968, when Robert Kennedy, the principal Democratic opponent of Hubert Humphrey (the eventual Presidential nominee) was assassinated.

However, conventions will continue to perform critical functions even if in the future every Presidential nomination is determined in the primary campaigns. Conventions "legitimize" the nominee, as Pulitzer Prize winning political writer David Broder has pointed out. "Someone can secure the nomination by plurality victories in the primaries," says Mr. Broder, "without being accepted by the majority of his own party. It is the acquiescence of others in the party—demonstrated at the convention hall—that tells the voters that the nominees are legitimately the party standard-bearers."

Another essential function of the convention is the election of the Vice-Presidential nominee. As we have seen, this cannot be done until after the President is officially chosen because, more often than not, the Vice-Presidential candidate is picked from among disappointed Presidential candidates. Most of them would not consent to run on the ticket until after it was made official that they do not have a chance to be President.

Finally, there is the approval of the party platform. Although it is largely ignored during the campaign, the press, if not the people, will continue to demand that a political party present some sort of written document that sets forth its program. And if it is to represent the party, then it must be approved by the party, and approval at a national convention is probably the most convincing method of "legitimizing" the party program.

The American system for nominating its Presidential and Vice-Presidential candidates is continually changing. And that, essentially, is what makes the American system so healthy. There is no need to tear down the system if the system itself can respond to change and the people's demands for improvement.

★ BIBLIOGRAPHY ★

Abels, Jules. *Out of the Jaws of Victory—The Astounding Election of 1948.* New York: Holt, Rinehart & Winston, 1959.

Boorstin, Daniel J. *The Genius of American Politics.* Chicago: University of Chicago Press, 1953.

Coyle, David Cushman. *The United States Political System and How it works.* New York: New American Library, 1954.

Democratic National Committee. *The Official Proceedings of the Democratic National Convention; 1976.* Washington: DNC, 1976.

Hoopes, Roy. *Getting With Politics.* New York: Delacorte, 1968.

The League of Women Voters. *Choosing the President.* Washington: LWV, 1976.

Liston, Robert A. *Politics: From Precinct to Presidency.* New York: Delacorte, 1968.

McGinniss, Joe, *The Selling of the President 1968.* New York: Trident Press, 1969.

Moos, Malcolm, and Hess, Stephen. *Hats in the Ring—the Making of Presidential Candidates.* New York: Random House, 1960.

Novak, Michael. *Choosing Our King.* New York: Macmillan, 1974.

Novak, Robert D. *The Agony of the GOP 1964.* New York: Macmillan, 1965.

Pearl, Arthur. *Landslide: The How and Why of Nixon's Victory (1972).* New Jersey: Citadel Press, 1973.

Polsby, Nelson W., and Wildavsky, Aaron B. *Presidential Elections*. 3rd ed. New York: Scribners, 1964.

Schlesinger, Arthur M., Jr. *The Coming to Power; Critical Presidential Elections in American History.* New York: McGraw-Hill, 1972.

Sorauf, Frank J. *Party Politics in America.* 2nd ed. Boston: Little, Brown, 1972.

U.S. News and World Report. *U.S. Politics Inside and Out.* Washington: U.S. News Publishing Co., 1970.

White, Theodore H. *The Making of the President 1960; 1964; 1968; 1972.* New York: Atheneum, 1961, 1965, 1969, 1973 (classic studies of four recent Presidential elections; 4 volumes).

★ INDEX ★

ABOUT ★ THE ★ AUTHOR

Roy Hoopes has been a political editor and writer for more than twenty-five years. He volunteered to work in his first Presidential campaign in 1956, and has been active along the campaign trail ever since. He is the author of more than eighteen books, most of them in the field of political science.

Mr. Hoopes is presently working, at home in Potomac, Maryland, on his next book for Franklin Watts on political campaigning.